More Teachers' Favorite Books for Kids

TEACHERS' CHOICES 1994 – 1996

INTERNATIONAL READING ASSOCIATION
800 Barksdale Road, PO Box 8139
Newark, Delaware 19714-8139, USA

TEACHERS' CHOICES
A project of the International Reading Association
Logo illustration by Chris Van Allsburg

The production of the Teachers' Choices lists that appear in this book involved many years of work by IRA's Teachers' Choices Committee. Many people in many different locations participated. The 1993–94 regional coordinators were Elaine Healy (Las Vegas, Nevada), Sandra J. Imdieke (Marquette, Michigan), Kate J. Kirby-Linton (Lithonia, Georgia), John Poeton (Barre, Vermont), Sam Sebesta (Seattle, Washington), Jane Wilkins (Des Moines, Iowa), and Sarah Womble (Sherwood, Arkansas); Donna Bessant (Monterey, California) coordinated the project. The 1994–95 regional coordinators were Melissa Rickey (Bellingham, Washington), Sandra J. Imdieke (Marquette, Michigan), Carol Lynch-Brown (Tallahassee, Florida), Virginia Schroder (Port Washington, New York), Sam Sebesta (Seattle, Washington), Jane Wilkins (Des Moines, Iowa), and Sarah Womble (Sherwood, Arkansas); Donna Bessant (Monterey, California) and Carole S. Rhodes (Brooklyn, New York) coordinated the project. The 1995–96 regional coordinators were Carol Brown (Corvallis, Oregon), Marci Mitchell (Mission, Texas), Vincent Hamman (Omaha, Nebraska), Carol Lynch-Brown (Tallahassee, Florida), Linda Graves (Pandora, Ohio), Melissa Rickey (Bellingham, Washington), and Virginia Schroder (Port Washington, New York); Carole S. Rhodes (Brooklyn, New York) coordinated the project.

The lists included in this publication first appeared in *The Reading Teacher*, a copyrighted journal of the International Reading Association.

ISBN 0-87207-179-0

Contents

Introduction

Chris Van Allsburg's logo, which appears opposite the contents page, vividly illustrates that Teachers' Choices are books that surprise us—they reach out and tap us on the shoulder to get our attention. These books introduce young students to ideas, issues, and questions that will set them on a path of exploration. Children and young adults will find in these stories an unexpected wonder—they will discover a better understanding of people and of themselves.

More Teachers' Favorite Books for Kids is an ideal guide for teachers who are seeking outstanding books that students can enjoy in the classroom. The books included in this volume were chosen because they reflect high literary quality in style, content, structure, beauty of language, and presentation. These are books that might not be discovered or fully appreciated by children without introduction by a knowledgeable adult. Teachers will appreciate these books for their potential for use across the curriculum in areas such as language arts, social studies, math, art, drama, and music. The books offer many opportunities for reading aloud, discussions, and writing.

Parents also will find *More Teachers' Favorite Books for Kids* a good source of suggestions for books to read aloud or share at home. Many titles provide background information on questions that arise from tours to a zoo, planetarium, or museum and from other shared family events.

Each year since 1989 the International Reading Association's Teachers' Choices project has identified outstanding U.S. trade books published for children and adolescents that teachers find to be exceptional in curriculum use. The selection is accomplished through a national field test of 200 to 500 newly published books submitted by U.S. trade-book publishers. Seven teams, made up of a regional coordinator, field leaders, teacher reviewers, and trainees for the project, try out the books in classrooms and libraries to identify those that meet established criteria. Regional coordinators circulate copies of the books among teachers and librarians to use with students. The coordinators record educators' reactions to each book and tabulate their final ratings. Every book is read by a minimum of 6 teachers or librarians in each region, although some books are read by as many as 200 people in a single region. Ratings from the 7 regions are collated to produce the national list, which is published in annotated form in the November issue of *The Reading Teacher* and is reproduced and widely circulated as a separate brochure.

This volume is a compilation of Teachers' Choices lists from 1994 to 1996. Included are descriptions of more than 80 books appropriate for children and young adults, complete with teachers' suggestions for curriculum use, as indicated by the symbol ❦. In order to make this book easier to use, books are grouped into Primary (grades K–2, ages 5–8), Intermediate (grades 3–5, ages 8–11), and Advanced (grades 6–8, ages 11–14) levels. Of course, these categories do overlap. Each entry includes bibliographic information about the book and an annotation; the Teachers' Choices list on which the book first appeared is indicated by the initials TC followed by the year. (Please note that the publishers' names and ISBNs refer to the original publications—hardcovers, except where indicated—evaluated at the test sites. In many cases, particularly for books from the earliest lists, paperback editions may now be available; in some cases, the original edition may be difficult to find or out of print. Librarians and bookstore employees should be able to provide current information on the availability of particular books. The bibliographic information here is provided simply as a starting point.) To increase the collection's usefulness as a resource tool, we have included indexes of titles, authors, and illustrators.

A special addition to this compilation is a supplement titled "Teachers' Choices in the Classroom." This supplement contains a collection of short articles written by teachers who have used Teachers' Choices books in their own classroom. These teachers also have been involved in the Teachers' Choices project and realize the value of using these books with their students.

This volume is a wonderful source for teachers, librarians, parents, grandparents, and young readers alike. Let *More Teachers' Favorite Books for Kids* surprise you. You'll discover some outstanding books for kids!

Primary Level

(Grades K–2)

All the Places to Love

Patricia MacLachlan. Illustrated by Mike Wimmer. Harper-Collins. ISBN 0-06-021098-2. TC '95.

A young boy, Eli, chronicles all the places and the people he loves on his family farm. The birth of his sister, Sylvie, signifies the continuity of life and the special qualities of the place she will know as home. "Where else," Eli tells her, "does an old turtle crossing the path make all the difference in the world?" Brightly colored paintings enhance the gently paced, lyrical text.

❦ As the book is read aloud, have students close their eyes and visualize the places Eli describes. Discuss the images and then study the detailed, realistic paintings. Another idea is to have students visualize all the places to love in their environment and create a mural of these images. Compare and contrast with Thomas Locker's *Family Farm* (1988).

Autumn Across America

Seymour Simon. Illustrated with photos. Hyperion.
ISBN 1-56282-467-8. TC '94.

> The beautiful photographs in this book vividly capture seasonal change from east to west across America. In words and pictures, Simon chronicles the changes in animals and plants as autumn advances.
>
> ❧ The photos are marvelous as creative writing prompts. Students can compare the desert in autumn to other parts of the United States or make a mural. Older students can further research the plants and animals mentioned in the book and write reports on what autumn signifies in other countries. Also appropriate for Intermediate.

Beatrix Potter

Alexandra Wallner. Illustrated by the author. Holiday House.
ISBN 0-8234-1181-8. TC '96.

> This chronological portrayal is cleverly illustrated, and it provides an interesting look at the life of a privileged but

Illustration ©1995 by Alexandra Wallner from Beatrix Potter. *Reprinted by permission of Holiday House.*

lonely girl who became a well-known author, illustrator, farmer, and gardener.

❧ A good story to share before reading any work by Potter. This book would fit well into a unit on self-esteem and would be valuable when dealing with issues of perspective (for example, the idea that wealth and fame do not necessarily eliminate loneliness).

Boundless Grace

Mary Hoffman. Illustrated by Caroline Binch. Dial. ISBN 0-8037-1715-6. TC '96.

This sequel to *Amazing Grace* reintroduces Grace, who receives an invitation from her father to travel to Africa where he lives with his new family. Once there, she enjoys the African food, clothing, and stories. Grace also feels the emotions of all children in families struggling through divorce and determines to write a story about families like hers when she returns home.

❧ An excellent tool for teachers and counselors who help children deal with understanding feelings and relationships. Students can write about their own heritage and family to create a book to share in a classroom family history museum. A family quilt could be created to integrate art and foster parental involvement.

The Bracelet

Yoshiko Uchida. Illustrated by Joanna Yardley. Philomel. ISBN 0-399-22503-X. TC '94.

The internment of Japanese Americans during World War II is a piece of U.S. history that has been overlooked in children's literature, with a few exceptions such as Uchida's writings. This moving tale, based on Uchida's own childhood, is one of friendship, loss, and growth. In it Emi learns that memories cannot be lost and that true friendships cannot be broken by distance.

❧ An excellent addition to any discussion of prejudice or stereotyping. The effects of racial propaganda in the United States against Japanese Americans might be compared to its effects in Germany against the Jews during World War II.

Valuable lessons on friendship and hope also are inherent in the book. Students will be able to identify with Emi's feelings and could begin their own stories of special friendships or the meaning of a personal talisman in times of trouble. Also appropriate for Intermediate and Advanced.

The Christmas Miracle of Jonathan Toomey

Susan Wojciechowski. Illustrated by P.J. Lynch. Candlewick. ISBN 1-56402-320-6. TC '96.

Poignant and beautifully illustrated, this book may well become a cherished Christmas classic. Readers discover why Mr. Toomey is known in town as "Mr. Gloomy" and watch a miracle unfold as the widow McDowell and her son guide him in carving the pieces for their new crèche.

🍎 The illustrations offer possibilities for studying early American life, and the text lends itself to making predictions and examining perspective. Teachers could encourage discussion about understanding and caring for others. An ideal Christmas read-aloud.

Dance of the Sacred Circle: A Native American Tale

Adapted and illustrated by Kristina Rodanas. Little, Brown. ISBN 0-316-75358-0. TC '95.

In the tradition of storytelling, Rodanas tells and beautifully illustrates this tale based on a legend from the Blackfeet people. In the tale a boy whose tribe is on the brink of starvation silently leaves camp in search of the Great Chief in the Sky. The boy finds the Chief, who gives him a special gift because of his bravery. The boy returns with the gift, which brings a renewed hope to his tribe and its descendants.

🍎 Have students read several different myths and compare and contrast. Experiment with text innovation: Have students rewrite the ending, substituting another gift that might help the tribe. Do a story map.

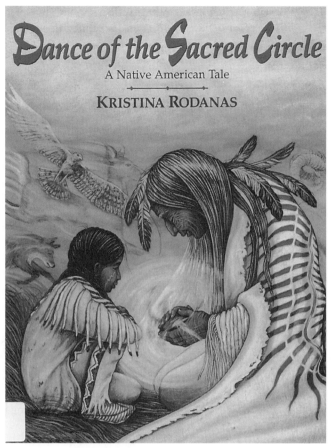

Jacket illustration ©1994 by Kristina Rodanas from Dance of the
Sacred Circle. *Reprinted by permission of Little, Brown and Company.*

Elephants Aloft
Kathi Appelt. Illustrated by Keith Baker. Harcourt Brace.
ISBN 0-15-225384-X. TC '94.

> Rama and Raja, two elephants, take an adventurous journey
> from India to Africa to visit their aunt. This is a colorful, well
> illustrated, easy book. One adjective on every two-page
> spread describes what is happening.
>
> 🐘 The following activities can be used after reading: text
> innovation, read and retell, and letter writing. This book is
> also a good introduction to antonyms. The illustrations could
> lead to comparing and discussing houses, animals, and weath-

er in different countries. A discussion of the differences between Indian and African elephants also could be initiated after reading *Elephants Aloft*.

Everglades
Jean Craighead George. Illustrated by Wendell Minor. HarperCollins. ISBN 0-06-021228-4. TC '96.

> A fascinating description of one of the world's unique ecosystems: the Florida Everglades. George carefully and accurately chronicles the evolution of this natural treasure.
>
> 🍎 The masterful paintings can be used to motivate students in art. Many social studies topics regarding social environments and the importance of cooperation among living creatures can be discussed after reading this book.

Grandad Bill's Song
Jane Yolen. Illustrated by Melissa Bay Mathis. Philomel. ISBN 0-399-21802-5. TC '95.

> When his grandfather dies, a young boy asks others how they feel, and then he shares his own feelings. Lyrically written and beautifully illustrated—a book for all ages.
>
> 🍎 An excellent tool for teachers and counselors who help children deal with death and with understanding feelings and relationships.

Grandfather's Journey
Allen Say. Illustrated by the author. Houghton Mifflin. ISBN 0-395-57035-2. TC '94.

> Have you ever wanted to be in two places at once? This account of the author's grandfather, who was born in Japan but grew up in America, reveals the yearning to return to another place and another time. Both cultures offer much to the boy who bridges two worlds. For children whose families move often, this book teaches how to adapt to change while continuing to cherish special memories.

🐛 Students could discuss how people keep memories of cultural backgrounds alive. Teachers could invite guests into the classroom to share pictures, stories, and memorabilia of other cultures. Also appropriate for Intermediate.

Here Is the Arctic Winter

Madeleine Dunphy. Illustrated by Alan James Robinson. Hyperion. ISBN 1-56282-336-1. TC '94.

A beautifully illustrated book about the endangered Arctic and the animals strong enough to survive the Arctic's cold and dark winter.

🐛 The lyrical, repetitive text is an excellent introduction to exploratory or informational text for beginning readers. Although labeled as a primary book, it could be used with intermediate and advanced readers in a study of the Arctic or endangered environments. Excellent for use across the curriculum.

John Henry

Julius Lester. Illustrated by Jerry Pinkney. Dial. ISBN 0-8037-1606-0. TC '95.

Based on the folk ballad, this book celebrates the life and "indomitable human spirit" of the legendary John Henry. Lester's dedication and accompanying notes provide a present-day context for this retelling. One reviewer stated, "Pinkney's illustrations are the perfect embellishment."

🐛 Find the sheet music or recordings of this ballad and have students sing along. Compare the versions of the song found in B.A. Botkin's *A Treasury of American Folklore* (1944) and Alan Lomax's *Folk Songs of North America* (1960) with Lester's retelling. Write a new stanza that tells where John Henry is buried: if not at the White House—as in Lester's version—then where?

Journey to Freedom: A Story of the Underground Railroad

Courtni C. Wright. Illustrated by Gershom Griffith. Holiday House. ISBN 0-8234-1096-X. TC '95.

> This narrative provides information about the Underground Railroad route followed by enslaved African Americans in the mid-1800s. Harriet Tubman guides 8-year-old Joshua and his family from slavery in the southern states to freedom in Canada. Joshua, as narrator, reveals the fear, hunger, and cold his family experiences before surviving the long journey.
>
> 🐛 Although listed as primary level, this book could be used at all grade levels. Students could respond in journals about how they would feel if they were Joshua, write a story about a journey they have made, or create a character poem.

The Library

Sarah Stewart. Illustrated by David Small. Farrar Straus Giroux. ISBN 0-374-34388-8. TC '96.

> Written in rhyme, this tale of Elizabeth Brown's love of books invites children to become lifelong readers. After showing how great libraries grow, Elizabeth eventually gives her own library of books to her community for everyone to enjoy.
>
> 🐛 In an age of technology, this refreshing story, full of rich language experiences, shares the magic of reading. The pen drawings that appear in contrast to Small's watercolors on each page will provoke class discussion. Students also will learn a different way to tell a story.

Illustration ©1995 by David Small from The Library *by Sarah Stewart. Reprinted by permission of Farrar Strauss & Giroux.*

Jacket illustration ©1995 by Chris K. Soentpiet from More Than Anything Else by Marie Bradby. Reprinted by permission of Orchard Books.

More Than Anything Else

Marie Bradby. Illustrated by Chris K. Soentpiet. Orchard. ISBN 0-531-09464-2. TC '96.

Nine-year-old Booker T. Washington wants to learn to read more than anything else. However, in 1865 in Malden, West Virginia, that is a difficult task. His family works in the saltworks all day, and this hard labor leaves little time to learn. Courage and determination enable him finally to pursue his dream.

🍎 The democratic process for human rights could be used as a topic for social studies when this book is read in class. Using a time line, continue to study Booker T. Washington and his life and document his accomplishments. Have students research other heroes and heroines on the Internet.

Only Opal: The Diary of a Young Girl

Opal Whiteley. Selected by Jane Boulton. Illustrated by Barbara Cooney. Philomel. ISBN 0-399-21990-0. TC '95.

This lyrical text documents the daily life of an orphan child growing up in an Oregon lumber camp during the early 19th century. Opal feels she is needed by her adopted parents only to help with the work load. Her sensitive feelings are revealed as she copes with her problems by meeting new people and sharing her love for nature.

🍎 Useful in language arts as students write in journals and diaries, perhaps about feelings and how to deal with sadness.

In social studies, students could compare and contrast pioneer spirit and life with today's challenges. For science, this book contains numerous nature topics including references to logging and ecology.

Our People

Angela Shelf Medearis. Illustrated by Michael Bryant. Atheneum. ISBN 0-689-31826-X. TC '95.

A father's stories about "our people" are retold by his daughter in this poetic text that captures the spirit and power of family oral traditions. Vibrant paintings illustrate this child's reflections as she plays a part in the glorious deeds of her African American ancestors. Her people built the pyramids, explored new lands, and emerged from slavery to become scientists, inventors, and "anything they wanted to be." All children will benefit from this tale of tradition, soaring esteem, and endless possibility.

❦ This personal journey through history will spark young readers' interest in the accomplishments of African Americans in various fields of endeavor. Teachers can model interviews of guest speakers in the classroom to trigger student interviews of family members and relatives. Students will be inspired to discuss and write the stories of their own heritage and may use this book as a pattern for personal histories.

Plane Song

Diane Siebert. Illustrated by Vincent Nasta. HarperCollins. ISBN 0-06-021464-3. TC '94.

In verse, Siebert reveals the wonders of flight and the many types of planes that cross our skies. Nasta's colorful and vivid illustrations enhance the explanations of what various planes do, from fire fighters to commuter jet props.

❦ Students will love the language of planes and pilots caught in the rhythm of the text. A useful addition to any discussion of flight, this book could spark research on different kinds of planes or the historical impact of the airplane. It also could be used in a unit on industry and machines. Children could replicate Siebert's style in books of their own about boats, trains, or trucks.

The Red Poppy

Irmgard Lucht. Illustrated by the author. Hyperion.
ISBN 0-7868-0055-0. TC '96.

> A multidimensional exploration of life cycles and forms in the habitat of a red poppy. Like the binocular microscope Lucht used to view and paint the poppy, her text and paintings create an encounter with nature enhanced by magnification.
>
> ❧ The vocabulary of plant physiology and reproduction become visual reality in this book, as students are introduced to natural environment study procedures. *The Red Poppy* includes examples of food chains, life cycles, and the use of microscopes and photography in scientific exploration. First

Jacket of The Red Poppy *by Irmgard Lucht used by permission of Hyperion Books for Children.*

published in Germany, this book also will familiarize children with international literature, geography, and the importance of natural events in social studies.

Sadako
Eleanor Coerr. Illustrated by Ed Young. Putnam.
ISBN 0-399-21771-1. TC '94.

"If a sick person folds one thousand paper cranes, the gods will grant her wish and make her well again." So 12-year-old Sadako, afflicted with leukemia caused by the atom bomb, began the task. Quiet prose and pastels commemorate her courage in this book, as does the statue of real-life Sadako in Hiroshima Peace Park at the top of the Mountain of Paradise.

🍎 This is a core book in one school's literature unit called "How Kids Face Trouble." More broadly, it might start a study of war's effect on individuals, a topic neglected in many history books. Students also could experiment with pastels to examine moods that artist Ed Young creates in this book and how he achieves these effects.

Tanya's Reunion
Valerie Flournoy. Illustrated by Jerry Pinkney. Dial.
ISBN 0-8037-1604-4. TC '96.

In this sequel to *The Patchwork Quilt*, young Tanya and her grandmother travel by bus to the family farm in Virginia. Tanya is not sure about farm life until she begins to understand the history that the farm holds.

🍎 This picture book presents a warm and loving African American family sharing the joys of a reunion. The story may provoke discussion on the desertion of the family farm for employment in cities. Because the pencil-and-watercolor illustrations effectively convey the affection that family members have for one another, teachers may want to include this book in thematic units on families.

Illustration ©1993 by Ed Martinez from Too Many Tamales *by Gary Soto. Reprinted by permission of G.P. Putnam's Sons.*

Too Many Tamales
Gary Soto. Illustrated by Ed Martinez. Putnam.
ISBN 0-399-22146-8. TC '94.

This book is a Christmas story, a Latino story, and a story that appeals to children all rolled into one. Maria tries on her mother's wedding ring while helping make tamales for Christmas, kneads the dough, and remembers the ring only after it is missing from her finger and the tamales are cooked.

Teachers can use this book with units that study families. The story shows how Latino traditions are integrated into cross-cultural celebrations like Christmas so that students can compare family traditions.

Tops & Bottoms
Adapted and illustrated by Janet Stevens. Harcourt Brace.
ISBN 0-15-292851-0. TC '96.

In this story it is hare versus bear, not hare versus tortoise! Hare turns out to be the victor in this tale of the power of industry over laziness. Hare talks Bear into becoming his vegetable business partner, and he even lets Bear choose which ends of the vegetables he will get—tops or bottoms. Eventually Hare's wit teaches Bear a lesson he needs to learn, and Bear never sleeps through planting season and harvest time again.

Students will love the illustrations and unusual sideways format of this book. It could be used to supplement a study of

vegetables and how they are grown. Students might enjoy
bringing vegetables to school for a "vegetable feast," leaving
intact the tops and bottoms.

Where Are You Going, Manyoni?

Catherine Stock. Illustrated by the author. Morrow.
ISBN 0-688-10352-9. TC '94.

Stock heightens the importance of Manyoni's journey by
painting the girl's tiny figure in glowing watercolors of the
vast African veld. Scrambling through the bush and over
plains, Manyoni introduces readers to an array of plantlife,
wildlife, and geographic features in Zimbabwe. Where does
Manyoni go on this momentous trek? Breathlessly reaching
her destination, Manyoni arrives at the village school to learn
and to play with her friends.

A picture glossary of wildlife and a pronunciation key to
unfamiliar words invite teachers to use this book for lessons
ranging from phonics to ecology. Word clues in the glossary
send children back through the pages in search of animals
they did not see. Learning to pronounce the new words helps
readers discover the rhyme and rhythm of the story's language—children love chiming "Matsheloni, Manyoni" as the
book is read aloud.

The Whispering Cloth: A Refugee's Story

Pegi Deitz Shea. Illustrated by Anita Riggio. Stitched by You Yang. Boyds Mills. ISBN 1-56397-134-8. TC '96.

This beautifully illustrated book tells the story of Mai, a war orphan who lives in a Thai refugee camp with her grandmother. To earn money, grandmother's widows' group creates pa'ndau story cloths. Working hard to perfect her sewing, Mai finds her own story to tell on her cloth—a tale of family love, loss, and hope for a brighter future.

🦋 This book could launch a social studies unit to show the customs and culture of Southeast Asia. Mai's story would enrich a study of communities around the world. Children fear war, and the book's message of hope and caring is a welcome one. Art teachers could share this book as an introduction to stitchery in the elementary grades; the idea of "sewing" a memoir would appeal to many students.

Jacket illustration ©1995 by Anita Riggio from The Whispering Cloth *by Pegi Deitz Shea. Reprinted by permission of Boyds Mills Press.*

Intermediate Level
(Grades 3–5)

The Always Prayer Shawl
Sheldon Oberman. Illustrated by Ted Lewin. Boyds Mills.
ISBN 1-878093-22-3. TC '95.

> In this cross-generational picture storybook, a young Jewish
> boy named Adam listens to stories of his grandfather's life.
> He inherits a prayer shawl from his ancestor in long-ago
> Russia and learns how he has inherited his namesake from
> his grandfather. This legacy, rich in tradition, provides a
> stable identity for each generation of grandsons in an ever-
> changing world.
>
> ❧ Have students describe what marks the passage of time in
> this book. Ask students to reflect on the traditions in their
> life: What changes and what remains the same? Also, students
> could interview family or friends about traditions in their life.
> Compile a book called "The Always Traditions" of the class.

Around the World in a Hundred Years: From Henry the Navigator to Magellan

Jean Fritz. Illustrated by Anthony Bacon Venti. Putnam.
ISBN 0-399-22527-7. TC '95.

Fritz makes early explorers such as Columbus, Vespucci, and
Magellan come alive with tales that are not forgotten. As
their ships sailed for the unknown, sailors were not sure if
they would be lost forever in a world of doom or come home
to their families. But their explorations of unknown lands (at
least from a European perspective) gave the world more accurate maps. Venti's illustrations help readers travel with these
brave men.

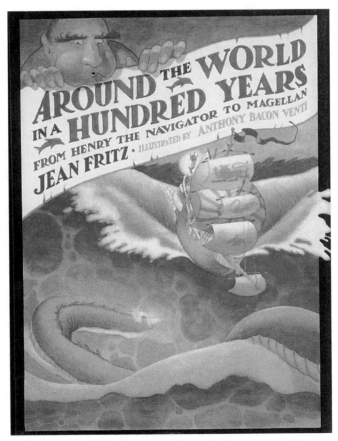

Jacket illustration ©1994 by Anthony Bacon Venti from Around the
World in a Hundred Years: From Henry the Navigator to Magellan
by Jean Fritz. Reprinted by permission of G.P. Putnam's Sons.

17

🍐 History can become more realistic as students enjoy the perspective of Fritz's humorous tales. As students examine early maps and notes from the author, they can discuss geography and early explorations with more specificity. The book is especially good for comparing maps from the 1400s with today's versions (from space, perhaps).

Baby
Patricia MacLachlan. Delacorte. ISBN 0-385-31133-8. TC '94.

In spare, almost poetic prose, MacLachlan relates the story of an abandoned baby who helps 12-year-old Larkin and her island family deal with their unspoken sadness.

🍐 *Baby* stresses the importance of relationships and communication among family members and offers opportunity for discussion and writing. For example, students could write letters to the baby's mother about how she is growing or letters that the mother might write back, or they could discuss whether Larkin kept a diary.

The Barn
Avi. Orchard. ISBN 0-531-06861-7. TC '95.

As Ben, his sister, and his brother build a barn on their farm in the Oregon Territory in 1855, Avi builds a story of family values and loyalty. Readers of all ages will be strengthened by the bravery, endurance, and hope that these children display while shouldering responsibilities for their ailing father. Any child who has ever dealt with the extended illness or death of a family member or friend will identify with these characters and their struggles.

🍐 This book is perfect for reading aloud and for use as a springboard to discussions of intergenerational relationships, responsibilities, and feelings. The book invites excursions into historical events relating to the time and place of the setting, and it provides teachers a great opportunity to inspire student writings.

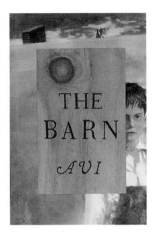

Jacket illustration ©1994 by Avi from The Barn. *Reprinted by permission of Orchard Books.*

The Big Book for Our Planet
Edited by Ann Durell, Jean Craighead George, and Katherine Paterson. Illustrations and photos from various sources. Dutton. ISBN 0-525-45119-6. TC '94.

> More than 40 stories, essays, poems, and limericks written and illustrated by popular authors and illustrators of children's books honor the planet Earth. As stated in the introduction, "This book says we can work with our planet, not against it."
>
> 🍃 This book offers innumerable cross-curricular possibilities: It introduces a variety of authors and illustrators, and it could be a springboard to numerous science and social studies topics. For language arts, have students compare and contrast stories and points of view or read and retell poems and write more. Appropriate for all ages.

Brown Honey in Broomwheat Tea
Joyce Carol Thomas. Illustrated by Floyd Cooper. Harper-Collins. ISBN 0-06-021087-7. TC '94.

> These poems are blank verse memories that reflect rural African American childhood, with paintings accompanying each poem. Many teachers singled out "Family Tree" as their favorite poem, adding praise for the exquisite, literal illustration on the facing page.

🍎 One teacher commented, "This collection of poems reflects love and continuity of family paired with an awareness of the African American experience, a poignant experience." Have students study an object or photo from their own life, and ask them to shape their impressions into blank verse and illustration to parallel the creative process behind this book.

Calling the Doves/El canto de las palomas
Juan Felipe Herrera. Illustrated by Elly Simmons. Children's Book Press. ISBN 0-89239-132-4. TC '96.

> Herrera lovingly recounts, in both Spanish and English, his early life in a migrant farm-working family. Images of night skies, bright mornings, and valley landscapes are richly drawn in both words and pictures. Stories full of poetry and tradition, told by warm and caring parents, provide the consistency and strong foundation from which the narrator looks back and remembers how he learned.
>
> 🍎 Use this book in a thematic unit on families to show a loving and respectful family relationship. For a unit on poetry writing, have students study the wonderful images. Children can create their own word images of their home or other memorable places, then illustrate them with bold, bright paints and pastels as in the book.

Celebrate America in Poetry and Art
Edited by Nora Panzer. Artwork from the National Museum of American Art, Smithsonian Institution. Hyperion. ISBN 1-56282-664-6. TC '95.

> Poetry celebrating more than 200 years of life and history is combined in this book with fine art from the collection of the National Museum of American Art. The poetry and visual art are divided into five themes, making for easy use.
>
> 🍎 The short biographical sketches of artists and poets are useful for either poetry or American art units. The book has wide appeal to many ages.

Christmas in the Big House, Christmas in the Quarters

Patricia C. McKissack and Fredrick L. McKissack. Illustrated by John Thompson. Scholastic. ISBN 0-590-43027-0. TC '95.

This book provides a look at not just a holiday, but a way of life: customs, recipes, poems, and songs celebrating Christmas in the big plantation houses and in the slave quarters before

Illustration ©1994 by John Thompson from Christmas in the Big House, Christmas in the Quarters by Patricia C. McKissack and Fredrick L. McKissack. Reprinted by permission of Scholastic Inc.

the U.S. Civil War. Dramatic illustrations offer windows into the period.

🍂 This book is a natural enhancement for social studies. The manner in which the book is written is a classic example of comparing and contrasting and suggests many similar activities for classes.

Dandelions
Eve Bunting. Illustrated by Greg Shed. Harcourt Brace. ISBN 0-15-200050-X. TC '96.

This is the story of a family moving from Illinois to Nebraska during the westward migrations in the United States. They travel across the plains in a covered wagon pulled by oxen, the father in search of a better life and opportunities for his family, and the wife and two daughters experiencing the emotions of leaving home, family, and memories behind. The dandelions are a metaphor for this family that endures the hardship of change.

🍂 This book could be used to make connections to social studies and the American westward migration. Students could write journal entries of what the children felt as they traveled west. They also could draw maps identifying the possible routes the family took or write personal narratives of times in their own life when they had to leave friends and memories to move to new places.

Dear Levi: Letters from the Overland Trail
Elvira Woodruff. Illustrated by Beth Peck. Knopf. ISBN 0-679-84641-7. TC '95.

While on a wagon train crossing the United States in 1851, orphaned Austin writes letters to his brother Levi whom Austin hopes to bring west some day. The letters trace the friendships, hardships, and fears of the journey. Accurate detail and description make the story believable.

🍂 Letters have been used historically as a medium to tell stories of family traditions, recipes, and history. Children might discover their own family stories from old letters and documents at home.

The Gettysburg Address
Abraham Lincoln. Illustrated by Michael McCurdy. Foreword by Garry Wills. Houghton Mifflin. ISBN 0-395-69824-3. TC '96.

> Masterful illustrations bring to life the immortal words of Abraham Lincoln's Gettysburg Address. A rich visual history helps young readers understand the depth of Lincoln's narrative.
>
> 🍎 This book presents creative writing opportunities, showing how a speech can become a book and a powerful piece of history. As a classroom resource, it can bring the historical record alive and ignite interest in the time period.

Gluskabe and the Four Wishes
Retold by Joseph Bruchac. Illustrated by Christine Nyburg Shrader. Cobblehill. ISBN 0-525-65164-0. TC '96.

> This Native American adventure is reminiscent of Aladdin or other tales in which wishes are granted. The story is told in various ways among the Wabanaki peoples of New England. Gluskabe, the helper of the Great Spirit, lives on a far-off island and will grant a wish to anyone who weathers the journey to him. Four Abenaki men attempt the challenge and face fierce storms and turbulent seas. Will they obey Gluskabe's instructions and receive their wishes? Brilliantly painted illustrations illuminate the fantastic journey. The story is entertaining and delivers a moral lesson.
>
> 🍎 Have students read different Native American tales and compare and contrast them with tales from other countries. They could create story maps and write their own versions of the four wishes in cooperative writing groups as they ponder the potential consequences for themselves and society.

Gooseberry Park
Cynthia Rylant. Illustrated by Arthur Howard. Harcourt Brace. ISBN 0-15-232242-6. TC '96.

> Kona, a Labrador retriever; Stumpy, a squirrel; Murray, a bat; and Gwendolyn, a hermit crab, courageously work together to avert disaster in Gooseberry Park.

❦ The importance of friendship echoes throughout this book. It could easily spark classroom dialogue and generate creative writing ideas such as stories about adventures students have had with their friends and times when a good friend would have been helpful in averting problems in their life.

The Great Migration: An American Story

Jacob Lawrence. Illustrated by author. With a poem "Migration" by Walter Dean Myers. HarperCollins. ISBN 0-06-023037-1. TC '94.

The text tells the story, but a powerful series of paintings conveys the essence of the early 20th-century movement of African Americans eager for employment in the industrial North.

❦ Children could investigate the migration of their own families: Where have families lived? What economic, social, or other factors motivate families to stay or move? Children may want to record their own family migration stories through a similar artistic sequence of panels.

Jacket illustration by Jacob Lawrence ©1993 by The Museum of Modern Art, New York, and The Phillips Collection, from The Great Migration. *Reprinted by permission of HarperCollins Publishers.*

Illustration ©1995 by Dom Lee from Heroes, *written by Ken Mochizuki. Reprinted by permission of Lee & Low Books.*

Heroes
Ken Mochizuki. Illustrated by Dom Lee. Lee & Low.
ISBN 1-880000-16-4. TC '96.

> Here is a view of World War II showing how the Asians and Pacific Islanders were treated in the United States after the war. In games at school, Donnie is always the enemy because he is Asian. Donnie's friends find out that all people may be heroes.
>
> 🐛 Use this book for a social studies unit on individual differences and prejudice. It also can be used for a study of Japan or a study of the problems of childhood. Companion resources include Eleanor Coerr's *Sadako* (1993) and Tatsuharu Kodama's *Shin's Tricycle* (1995).

Hiding Out: Camouflage in the Wild
James Martin. Illustrated with photos by Art Wolfe. Crown.
ISBN 0-517-59392-0. TC '94.

> Superb photographs make this a book for all ages. Both the text and pictures graphically explore how animals use camouflage for survival. Includes an easy-to-read index.

🍎 Teachers reviewing this book felt it was essential to use with their science unit on animals. Students can do a real hands-on activity using this book as a resource.

Jacob's Rescue: A Holocaust Story

Malka Drucker and Michael Halperin. Bantam. ISBN 0-553-08976-5. TC '94.

> Eight-year-old Jacob and his relatives, forced to live in the Warsaw Ghetto, are starving and waiting for deportation to the Nazi death camps. Risking their own lives, a Polish family takes Jacob and his brother and hides them.
>
> 🍎 Use this book to study the Holocaust along with others depicting humanitarian efforts during World War II, such as *Rescue: The Story of How Gentiles Saved Jews in the Holocaust* by Milton Meltzer (1991) and *Number the Stars* by Lois Lowry (1989). Some students may want to draw pictures of Jacob's dark, cramped hiding places and then write about how they would feel in Jacob's situation. Also appropriate for Advanced.

Kate Shelley: Bound for Legend

Robert D. San Souci. Illustrated by Max Ginsburg. Dial. ISBN 0-8037-1289-8. TC '96.

> San Souci presents the true story of Kate Shelley as she courageously seeks help for the people trapped in a wrecked train during a storm. This story does not end after Kate's heroic deed: It continues as she makes contributions to society as an adult.
>
> 🍎 Students could pursue a unit on young women in America or abroad. Encourage them to write articles for local newspapers about heroic people they know.

Kinaaldá: A Navajo Girl Grows Up

Monty Roessel. Illustrated with photos by the author. Foreword by Michael Dorris. Lerner. ISBN 0-8225-2655-7. TC '94.

> The Kinaaldá is the traditional coming of age ceremony for Navajo women. Photographs and a descriptive text help read-

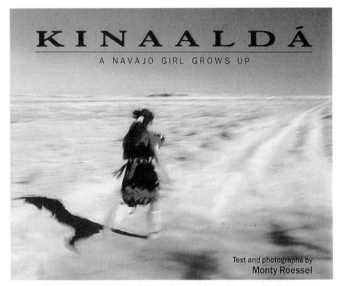

ers vicariously experience the corncake baking, prayers, and races that are part of the tradition. The ancient ceremony, viewed from a contemporary perspective, clarifies and affirms the values of the Navajo people.

After reading the legend "Changing Woman," which is retold in this book, students will want to learn about other Native American legends. Learning about coming of age traditions from other cultures is another natural extension.

Lives of the Musicians: Good Times, Bad Times (and What the Neighbors Thought)

Kathleen Krull. Illustrated by Kathryn Hewitt. Harcourt Brace. ISBN 0-15-248010-2. TC '94.

> The humor in the title of this book reverberates throughout 20 brief but pointed biographical sketches of diverse musicians (such as Johann Sebastian Bach, George Gershwin, and Clara Schumann). As readers learn about what the musicians ate, their bad habits, and other foibles, they begin to understand the significance of their lives and music.

🐦 Music teachers can read the story of a musician in this book prior to playing the music, which will intrigue students. Further interest in learning about these musicians and their times also may be generated.

Misoso: Once Upon a Time Tales from Africa
Retold by Verna Aardema. Illustrated by Reynold Ruffins. Apple Soup/Knopf. ISBN 0-679-83430-3. TC '95.

Verna Aardema has gathered and retold 12 entertaining "misoso" (once upon a time) tales from Africa. The tales are arranged geographically, and readers need only turn a page to take a literary jaunt across the continent. The poetry and musical language facilitate reading aloud, and the powerful illustrations convey the humor and flair of the artist and storyteller. Glossaries, a map, and informative source notes provide further insight into African history and tradition.

🐦 Students will love the rhythm and language of the text. Children can interview family members and write and retell folk tales from their ethnic and geographic heritages. Social studies connections can be made with a deeper understanding of Africa's geography.

My Painted House, My Friendly Chicken, and Me
Maya Angelou. Illustrated with photos by Margaret Courtney-Clarke. Clarkson Potter. ISBN 0-517-59667-9. TC '95.

This is a colorful and delightful portrait of the South African Ndebele culture and the influences of modern life upon its artwork. As Thandi describes life in her village, readers can marvel at the intricate wall paintings and beadwork that are the signature of the Ndebele and can understand Thandi's pride in her family.

🐦 Children could compare the differences in cultures through a Venn diagram. In a unit on friendship, the value of trust could be emphasized through Thandi's relationship with her pet chicken. This book also would be helpful in developing multicultural understandings by using the wonderful photographs to inspire colorful paintings depicting students' own families celebrating their special moments. A fine addition to any study of family relationships and heritage.

From My Painted House, My Friendly Chicken, and Me *by Maya Angelou, photographs by Margaret Courtney-Clarke. ©1994 by Maya Angelou and Margaret Courtney-Clarke. Reprinted by permission of Random House, Inc.*

Night of the Full Moon
Gloria Whelan. Illustrated by Leslie Bowman. Knopf.
ISBN 0-679-84464-3. TC '94.

Libby is a daughter in an 1840s family who live on the Michigan frontier near Potawatomi Indians. In this era of westward expansion, the tribe and Libby's friend Taw-cum-e-go-qna (Fawn) face evacuation from their land.

🍂 This book may be useful in studies about the westward movement and its effects on Native Americans, ecology, and growth of the United States. It can be compared with Betsy C. Byars's *Trouble River* (1989) or Elizabeth G. Speare's *Sign of the Beaver* (1905).

The Other Alice: The Story of Alice Liddell and Alice in Wonderland

Christina Björk. Illustrated by Inga-Karin Eriksson. R & S Books. ISBN 91-29-62242-5. TC '94.

Charles Dodgson's friendship with Alice Liddell, who was 20 years younger than he, produced animated conversations, puzzles, mazes, and photos, which are generously laid out on the pages in this book. The artifacts give readers the beginnings of *Alice's Adventures in Wonderland*, including the real

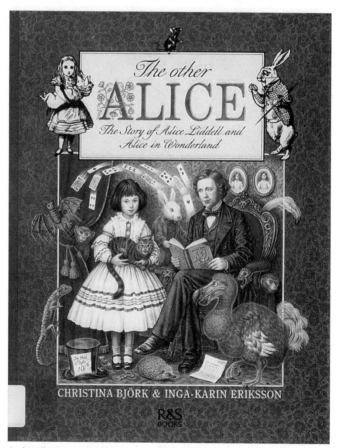

Jacket illustration ©1993 by Inga-Karin Eriksson from The Other Alice: The Story of Alice Liddell and Alice in Wonderland *by Christina Björk. Reprinted by permission of Farrar Strauss & Giroux.*

story of the dodo and the accidental arrival of a hedgehog at a croquet game. ("In the Antipodes they always play croquet with hedgehogs," said Mr. Dodgson.)

🦋 Use this book for literature study: With students, discover how snippets of reality, written or photographed and remembered, transform into a work of imagination. It also could be used in a unit on fantasy that features Lewis Carroll. Contact Societies for Alice and Carroll Friends, whose addresses are included in the book. Also appropriate for Advanced.

Paint and Painting
Adapted by Jeannie Hutchins. Illustrations from various sources. Scholastic. ISBN 0-590-47636-X. TC '95.

> This compact spiral-bound part of the "Voyages of Discovery" series appeals to the sense of touch as well as sight. It includes a prehistoric cave painting on heavy paper as rough and irregular as stone, a swatch of real papyrus masking ancient Egyptian figures, a perfectly photographed watercolor paint box that tells almost everything about the artist who used it, and doors that open to medieval and modern masterworks. A glossary, time line, and list for further reading accompany a succinct text that invites readers to be part of the art of painting.
>
> 🦋 Use this book to begin a study of painting—it gives schema and motivation to research art of each historical period. Invite students to extrapolate, to describe, or to create paintings for the 21st century.

Powwow
George Ancona. Illustrated with photos by the author. Harcourt Brace. ISBN 0-15-263268-9. TC '94.

> This photo essay of the largest powwow held in the United States, the Crow Fair, provides a view of the friendship and traditions shared at the event held in Crow Agency, Montana. It explains four distinct dance categories through text and photos and conveys a sense of the importance of the dance celebrations in the lives of Native Americans.
>
> 🦋 This book is an excellent source for an introduction to Native American customs. The powwow in this book could be compared with gatherings of other tribes and with celebrations of other cultures.

Star of Fear, Star of Hope
Jo Hoestlandt. Illustrated by Johanna Kang. Walker.
ISBN 0-8027-8373-2. TC '96.

When the Nazis occupied Paris during World War II, Lydia
had to wear a yellow star on her coat. While celebrating the
ninth birthday of Lydia's best friend, Helen, the girls are
frightened in the middle of the night by two people—also
wearing stars on their coats—hiding to avoid arrest by the
Nazis. Lydia leaves the celebration immediately to warn her
parents. Intermediate children can appreciate Helen's resent-
ment at being abandoned by her friend and Lydia's courage
and loyalty to her family.

🍂 This true story gives students an honest but gentle introduction to the horrors of the Holocaust through the eyes of a
child. It also provides a view of the politics and geography
associated with the time. First published in French, this book
may be used to introduce children to international literature
and the value of translated books in understanding history,
other cultures, and the universality of human experiences.

Stranded at Plimoth Plantation 1626
Gary Bowen. Illustrated by the author. HarperCollins.
ISBN 0-06-022541-6. TC '95.

Stunning woodcuts bring early American history to life in
this journal of a boy shipwrecked at Plimoth. One reader's
description follows: "The illustrations are the highest point.
They develop and become more sophisticated as the character learns to use color and develops his woodblock skills."

🍎 Students can research and write their own fictitious diaries about living in an early American settlement. Using art gum erasers or other art materials, students can create their own block prints to capture the process used in this book.

The Third Planet: Exploring the Earth from Space
Sally Ride and Tam O'Shaughnessy. Illustrated with photos from the National Aeronautics & Space Administration. Crown. ISBN 0-517-59361-0. TC '95.

> With spectacular photographs taken from space, the knowledgeable authors of this book provide a unique visual perspective of the Earth's landforms and weather. Readers look down into the eye of a hurricane, see an infrared composite of the Gulf Stream, and learn where the ocean's plankton is most bountiful.
>
> 🍎 Students will be drawn into the photographs and concise text. This book supports studies of the atmosphere, the greenhouse effect, geology, the environment, and the visible impact of human life on Earth.

The True Adventure of Daniel Hall
Diane Stanley. Illustrated by the author. Dial. ISBN 0-8037-1468-8. TC '96.

> In 1856, 14-year-old Daniel Hall sets sail from New Bedford, Massachusetts, on a whaling ship bound for arctic waters. Two years of hardship and cruelty imposed by a moody and violent ship captain cause Daniel to desert the ship in Siberia, where he has many exciting adventures in his struggle to survive.
>
> 🍎 The ship's itinerary is traced on a world map throughout the book, which makes this true adventure an excellent tool for teaching geography. A study of the history of whaling and 19th-century life aboard a ship would be enhanced by the vivid illustrations in this book.

The Well
Mildred D. Taylor. Dial. ISBN 0-8037-1802-0. TC '96.

This story, set in Mississippi, recalls the deep south in the United States in the early part of the 20th century. It tells of racial prejudice and rivalry that erupted when all the local water sources dried up—except for the well on the Logan farm. For many white families in the area, this is a time to let bygones be bygones, but it causes the Simms to beg for water from a black family. Hammer Logan's fierce pride and Charlie Simms's meanness combine to cause near disaster for every family in the area.

🍎 This book is a wonderful addition to an author study of Mildred Taylor and will deepen understanding of bigotry and racial bias. Clear and descriptive language make it an ideal model for character study and for how an author shows, rather than tells, characters' feelings. Young David Logan tells the story, and teachers could use this book to show the effectiveness of a first-person narrative.

Advanced Level
(Grades 6–8)

Anne Frank: Beyond the Diary
Ruud van der Rol and Rian Verhoeven. Illustrated with photos. Introduction by Anna Quindlen. Viking. ISBN 0-670-84932-4. TC '94.

> Historical essays, diary excerpts, and interviews, accompanied by photographs, illustrations, and maps, provide a deeper insight into the upheaval that tore apart Anne Frank's world. This book makes Anne more of a real person, not just someone students read about.
>
> ❦ Middle school teachers who received and used this book in their classroom felt it was the key piece in their unit on the Holocaust, and many of the students had trouble putting it down.

Buffalo Gals: Women of the Old West
Brandon Marie Miller. Illustrated with photographs. Lerner. ISBN 0-8225-1730-2. TC '96.

> This book chronicles the history of pioneer women who traveled with their families to the American West. Readers learn how women crossed the plains, set up house, and won the

right to vote in western states and territories. Through journal entries, song lyrics, and letters home, the women tell their special stories of courage, spirit, and adventure.

🐚 An excellent source for primary research into the westward movement from a feminine point of view. Students can divide the chapters and, in cooperative research groups, study the time period, geography, and characters. Invite students to find songs of the period to sing or to cook food representative of the era.

Jacket illustration ©1995 by Brandon Marie Miller from Buffalo Gals: Women of the Old West. *Reprinted by permission of Lerner Publications.*

Bull Run

Paul Fleischman. Illustrated by David Frampton. Harper-Collins. ISBN 0-06-021446-5. TC '94.

> How many versions of the U.S. Civil War could be gathered by interviewing eyewitnesses? Fleischman has created the voices of 16 eyewitnesses to the Civil War's first great battle at Bull Run including a reluctant general, a fervent black freeman, a disillusioned doctor, a sketch artist, an 11-year-old fife player, and a horse lover. In two-page chapters, the author weaves these firsthand accounts together to give a chilling picture of war between neighbors.
>
> 🐞 Teachers might use this book in a Readers Theatre style, making history come alive in the classroom with props and costumes. Other uses might imitate the narrative style by fictionalizing other historic events with multiple viewpoints.

Catherine, Called Birdy

Karen Cushman. Clarion. ISBN 0-395-68186-3. TC '95.

> One year in the life of spunky 13-year-old Birdy, daughter of an English country knight, is told through her diary entries. Readers will enjoy learning about life in a medieval manor—complete with fleas, cow dung, and stomach problems for the inhabitants. Birdy's father seeks ways to marry her off profitably, while Birdy irrepressibly thwarts his efforts through devious plots!
>
> 🐞 This work of historical fiction is a wonderful read-aloud that can reveal the everyday lives of people in the Middle Ages and spark further study of this period. In addition, Birdy's humorous and earthy diary entries present universal truths about growing up.

Champions: Stories of Ten Remarkable Athletes

Bill Littlefield. Illustrated by Bernie Fuchs. Foreword by Frank Deford. Little, Brown. ISBN 0-316-52805-6. TC '94.

> These short biographical sketches of 10 female and male athletes focus on their perseverance in reaching both their sports and personal goals. A list of suggested readings is included.
>
> 🐞 These stories can lead to discussion of personal values and overcoming obstacles. Some teachers have used the

biographies to discuss courage and prejudice, which later became part of a unit on careers. Have students write plays, Readers Theatre scripts, or newspaper articles about the athletes or develop time lines. Also appropriate for Intermediate.

Cut from the Same Cloth: American Women of Myth, Legend, and Tall Tale

Robert D. San Souci. Illustrated by Brian Pinkney. Introduction by Jane Yolen. Philomel. ISBN 0-399-21987-0. TC '94.

This collection of 20 authentic folk stories about legendary American women provides a wonderful balance for the traditional American heroic tales about men. The stories, ideal for reading aloud, are arranged by five regions—Northeast, South, Midwest, Southwest, and West—and include tales of African Americans, Native Americans, Anglo-Americans, and Mexican Americans, as well as stories from Hawaii and Alaska.

🍃 Compare the exploits of Molly Cottontail with those of her male counterpart, Peter Rabbit, or learn about Mike Fink's daughter, Sal, as chronicled in newspapers in the early 1840s. Also appropriate for Intermediate.

Jacket illustration ©1993 by Brian Pinkney from Cut From the Same Cloth *by Robert D. San Souci. Reprinted by permission of Philomel Books.*

The Dream Keeper and Other Poems
Langston Hughes. Illustrated by Brian Pinkney. Knopf.
ISBN 0-679-84421-X. TC '95.

These poems by Hughes were originally published in 1932, but this new edition includes an additional seven of his poems, along with Pinkney's scratchboard illustrations. Although it is a book for children, it also can be enjoyed by readers of all ages.

An excellent introduction to an author study; although best known for his poetry, Hughes has published works in all forms of literature. Students could write poems to be compiled into a class book of poetry.

The Eagle Kite
Paula Fox. Orchard. ISBN 0-531-06892-7. TC '96.

The truth has haunted Liam for three years, but he keeps it to himself. Liam's father has AIDS. A poignant story of dealing with death and its ramifications.

This is a resource for introducing the issue of HIV/AIDS education. It contains numerous opportunities for discussions and debates among groups. This book also is a natural for guest speakers and for informing students about health concerns and the ways the virus is spread.

Earthshine
Theresa Nelson. Orchard. ISBN 0-531-06867-6. TC '95.

Twelve-year-old Slim has dealt with her parents' divorce, her father's homosexuality, and now his impending death from AIDS. She faces this tragedy with the help of a support group that gives her information, friendship, and courage. One classroom teacher wrote, "This book deals with AIDS, homosexuality, and death in a real way without shock tactics. It's beautiful, gentle, and even funny." Another teacher stated, "The content is volatile but carefully executed so as to present many sides of the same issue."

Relate this title to study and discussion of current health-related issues in society. Have students research the statistics and demographics of AIDS. How does the information in this book compare to information provided in the health curricu-

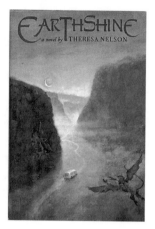

Jacket illustration ©1994 by Theresa Nelson from Earthshine. *Reprinted by permission of Orchard Books.*

lum? Research support groups that are in the community for people who face life-threatening or chronic illness. Have students gather information about a health issue of concern to them and create an informational display, or have them keep a journal, like Slim does, as they read this book.

For Home and Country: A Civil War Scrapbook
Norman Bolotin and Angela Herb. Illustrated with photographs. Lodestar. ISBN 0-525-67495-0. TC '96.

This is a factual, pictorial account of average people's lives during the U.S. Civil War. The use of comments from diaries and letters reflects an overview of the war from both civilians and soldiers. Special features of the book are the time line, glossary, and selected bibliography, which contains outstanding resources.

❦ Children will eagerly explore both pictures and text because of the focus on everyday living. Writing skills could be pursued by having students compose journals and letters. Students may want to explore the Internet to find more photos and text about the Civil War.

The Giver

Lois Lowry. Houghton Mifflin. ISBN 0-395-64566-2. TC '94.

Jonas has been chosen as receiver and keeper of a futuristic community's memories. As he learns about the joys of color in the world and the horror of war, Jonas begins to question the rules in this ideal world. He makes a choice about his own future, but the outcome is left for readers to decide.

🍂 Unsettling yet unforgettable questions are raised in this novel. Mature readers must ponder choices between freedom and sameness, the consequences of our choices, and our vision of what makes a perfect society. The ideas in this book challenge the thinking of both children and teachers when they explore critical questions together. If one of literature's purposes is to better understand our beliefs and values, this novel delivers.

Hiding to Survive: Stories of Jewish Children Rescued from the Holocaust

Maxine B. Rosenberg. Illustrated with photographs. Clarion. ISBN 0-395-65014-3. TC '95.

First-person accounts of horrors witnessed show how the will to survive and their rescuers' courage sustained children who escaped the Holocaust. Postscripts portray what became of these children as adults, reminding us of possibilities denied nonsurvivors. Commented one reader, "These narratives add a dimension of hope often left out of the discussion of genocide."

🍂 Use this book to study the Holocaust, along with Susan D. Bachrach's *Tell Them We Remember* (Teachers' Choice 1995). Students could research what their grandparents remember of war, what hardships they endured, and what changes war made in their lives. They could write a newspaper or journal, construct a mural, or create a class book similar to this one.

Julie

Jean Craighead George. Illustrated by Wendell Minor.
HarperCollins. ISBN 0-06-023528-4. TC '95.

This sequel is worthy of its predecessor *Julie of the Wolves*, a
winner of the Newbery Medal. Julie who has lived in harmony with a wolfpack for many months must now try to adjust
to modern ways that her father has adopted. He has remar-
ried, is a leader of his village's corporation, and, worst of all, is
determined to shoot Julie's wolves if they threaten the village
industry, the breeding of uminmak or musk oxen. Julie's
dilemma intensifies when she enounters a handsome young
man from Siberia who hopes to win her heart but wants her
to stay true to the old ways.

🐾 Once more George brings to the attention of readers the
need for all beings to live in harmony with one another by
sharing the earth. The settings are vividly described and the
conflicts are strongly felt by readers in this book. It is an
excellent resource for studying the Alaskan Eskimo culture,
life on the tundra, wildlife, and ecology.

*Jacket illustration ©1994 by Wendell
Minor from* Julie *by Jean Craighead
George. Reprinted by permission of
HarperCollins Publishers.*

Lincoln

Edited by Milton Meltzer. Illustrated by Stephen Alcorn.
Harcourt Brace. ISBN 0-15-245437-3. TC '94.

> Through a wonderful combination of biographical commentary and Abraham Lincoln's speeches, letters, and writings, historian Meltzer presents the 16th President of the United States.
>
> ❦ This is an obvious source for units dealing with the Civil War, biography in general, presidential life, life in the 1800s, and related topics. It makes a great read-aloud, and it could be the focus for cooperative group studies around specific periods of Lincoln's life.

Lives of the Artists: Masterpieces, Messes (and What the Neighbors Thought)

Kathleen Krull. Illustrated by Kathryn Hewitt. Harcourt
Brace. ISBN 0-15-200103-4. TC '96.

> Krull offers 20 short biographical sketches of famous artists in which fascinating information is shared with humor and pathos. Captivating pictures of the artists along with intriguing facts about their most famous works are included.
>
> ❦ The anecdotal appeal of the sketches may tempt reluctant students to do more in-depth research about selected artists. This book could provide a model for writing biographies or autobiographies that really interest readers. Opportunities abound for integrating historical, cultural, and gender issues.

Lives of the Writers: Comedies, Tragedies (and What the Neighbors Thought)

Kathleen Krull. Illustrated by Kathryn Hewitt. Harcourt
Brace. ISBN 0-15-248009-9. TC '95.

> As readers become more proficient and independent in their book choices, they often wonder about the lives of the authors. Krull's treasury of anecdotes and sketches of 20 well-known authors offers a peek into their histories, whether comic or tragic, ordinary or extraordinary. The "Bookmarks" that follow each piece highlight a particular work, giving an insight into its publication. Hewitt's caricatures enhance the

text and bring the writers to life. This book is an ideal companion to any collection of the classics.

🍎 *Lives of the Writers* offers another way of presenting life stories. It could encourage students to seek information about other favorite authors and create their own anthologies. As a prereading strategy, students could learn about authors' lives and then look for the influences on their writing as they read. Children could write autobiographical sketches and reflect on the impact of their lives on their own writing. The book also is a stepping stone to more complete biographies and further exploration of these authors' works.

Make Lemonade
Virginia Euwer Wolff. Holt. ISBN 0-8050-2228-7. TC '94.

Knowing that she has to start saving money for college, 14-year-old Verna LaVaughn responds to an advertisement for a babysitter. What she discovers about herself and the 17-year-old mother of two babies who become her family are lessons in determination and caring, and a willingness to take risks to succeed. The story, written in text lines that break at natural speaking phrases, is both captivating and haunting for the mature reader.

🍎 This book could generate discussion and response about life's significant issues while portraying hopeful solutions to problems. Teachers can use the slogan "Making lemonade when life gives you lemons" as a theme for thoughtful, personal response and for genuine problem solving with teenagers.

Malcolm X: By Any Means Necessary
Walter Dean Myers. Illustrated with photos. Scholastic. ISBN 0-590-46484-1. TC '94.

Beginning with the first chapter titled "The Father," readers get a broad overview of the 1960s U.S. civil rights advocate Malcolm X. The book provides detailed chronological information and describes events during his lifetime from 1925 to 1965. It includes a lengthy bibliography for further information.

After reading this book, follow-up activities might include a comparison of civil rights leaders during the 1960s, discussion of fact versus opinion, comparison of this book with the Spike Lee movie on Malcolm X, and development of a time line.

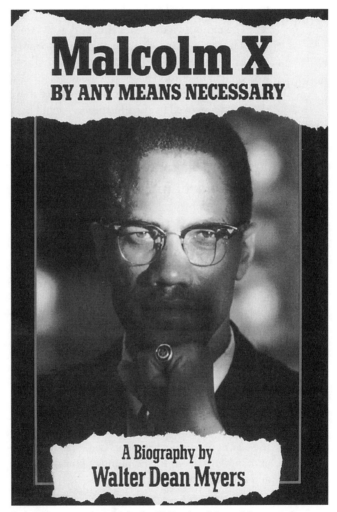

Jacket illustration from Malcolm X: By Any Means Necessary by Walter Dean Myers ©1993. Reprinted by permission of Scholastic Inc.

The Middle Passage: White Ships, Black Cargo
Tom Feelings. Introduction by John Henrik Clarke. Dial.
ISBN 0-8037-1804-7. TC '96.

A powerful pictorial essay depicts the slave trade from the
African coast to the Americas. The illustrations are passion-
ately moving and leave readers with a deep understanding of
the gruesome ordeal suffered by enslaved Africans.

❦ The most obvious use for this work is in American and
world history courses when tracing the history of slavery. The
quality and strength of the black-and-white illustrations
would elicit discussion about the use of color versus mono-
chromatic drawings in an art class. Response in writing to
the feelings evoked by the illustrations would be a suitable
English class application.

On the Wings of Peace: Writers and Illustrators Speak Out for Peace, in Memory of Hiroshima and Nagasaki
Compiled by Sheila Hamanaka. Illustrations from various
sources. Clarion. ISBN 0-395-72619-0. TC '96.

This is an outstanding anthology of prose and poetry about
the horror of war and violence. Strong language and vivid
images make the book best suited for older students. Never-
theless, the message it carries should not be forgotten, and
the book is a must for those who teach peace.

❦ Use this compilation to supplement the study of any period of war or conflict (such as in Palestine, Bosnia, or inner-
city ghettos). Students could search for the common threads
that weave stories of war together, regardless of when they
occurred. Their observations would contribute to compelling
arguments about peace efforts or spark further investigation of
the causes of conflict. Students could research information
and opinions about the bombing of Hiroshima and Nagasaki
and then debate the decisions.

Phoenix Rising

Karen Hesse. Holt. ISBN 0-8050-3108-1. TC '95.

After a nuclear power plant disaster, Nyle's Gran chooses to shelter two ill refugees on her Vermont farm. Fearful of death and the dying, Nyle eventually faces the effects and the reality of the disaster with courage and compassion.

❦ A reviewer asked, "How do any of us really know what the worldwide lasting effects of an accident would be or how we would personally react?" This book helps readers explore and discuss issues we hope never to face.

Red-Tail Angels: The Story of the Tuskegee Airmen of World War II

Patricia and Fredrick McKissack. Illustrated with photographs. Walker. ISBN 0-8027-8292-2. TC '96.

The awe-inspiring achievements of the Tuskegee Airmen of World War II have finally become part of recorded American history. These wartime aviators, known as the Red-Tail Angels because of the red markings on their aircraft tails, struggled for acceptance and paved the way for future generations of African American flight crews. The McKissacks tell the Angels' glorious story, chronicle their difficulties, and explain that the country they defended—plagued by segregation—refused to acknowledge their heroism. Superb photography adds interest and brings this phenomenal story to life.

❦ This work is an excellent choice for a general study relating to World War II, black history, or aviation. Each student could explore one seemingly impossible dream and write about how to accomplish it against all odds, then they could share their dreams with classmates.

Rosie the Riveter: Women Working on the Home Front in World War ll

Penny Colman. Illustrated with photographs. Crown. ISBN 0-517-59790-X. TC '96.

Rosie the Riveter is the story of the women of 1943 in America who became welders, riveters, crane operators, railroad workers, bus drivers, typists, farm workers, and assembly line workers—women who were needed in almost any job to fight World War II from the home front. The book explains how women chose their jobs, how their husbands felt, how their lives were changed, and how the tapestry of the American work force changed forever. An added bonus are more than 60 archival black-and-white photos, famous posters, and advertisements of the period.

❦ Read this book as an excellent introduction to research into women's roles in the work force since World War II and the issue of equity in terms of salary and promotion. How did women's salaries compare with men's in 1943? How do they compare today? A debate on the issue of equity in employment will foster higher level thinking, and students can create graphs and charts to illustrate their points and integrate math skills.

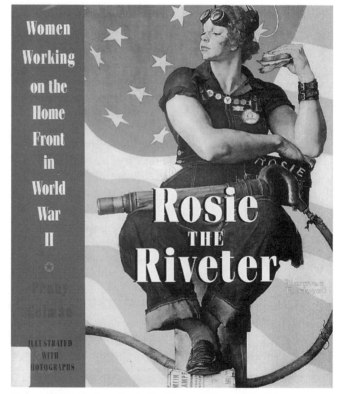

Jacket photography from Rosie the Riveter: Women Working on the Home Front in World War II, *courtesy of the Norman Rockwell Museum at Stockbridge. Printed by permission of the Norman Rockwell Trust. ©1943 the Norman Rockwell Trust.*

Ship

David Macaulay. Illustrated by the author. Houghton Mifflin. ISBN 0-395-52439-3. TC '94.

The genius of artist David Macaulay is that he looks closely at his subject and transmits the excitement of his scrutiny to readers young and old. The modern first half of the book shows how scientists assemble evidence of a 16th-century wooden caravel sunk off a reef in the Caribbean. The historical second half, a fictitious diary, describes the building of that ship, the *Magdalena*, and the hopes and plans of its owners.

❧ This book will enliven the study of exploration, with its clear parallel between 16th-century shipbuilding craft and today's hard effort to uncover the past. Based on evidence here, students can write or dramatize what happened to the *Magdalena* when it encountered a storm off the Bahamas and met the "voracious appetite of the murderous reef."

Spirit Walker

Nancy Wood. Illustrated by Frank Howell. Doubleday. ISBN 0-385-30927-9. TC '94.

In the preface to *Spirit Walker*, poet Nancy Wood explains what it took for her as an outsider to understand the beliefs of the Taos Pueblo Indians: "Learning to listen...letting go of old, worn-out cultural ideas...and solitude." These qualities permeate the text. Drawing on the cultural traditions of the Taos people, the poems and accompanying paintings create a caring and illuminating picture of these unique people who still hold their place in the modern world. In turn, readers come to understand the world and themselves a little better.

❧ Have students listen to the poems more than once. What images are evoked? Students may want to create these images with paints. Compare the myths, legends, and traditions of the Taos Pueblo Indians with other Native American cultures; discuss similar stories, different traditions, and how these are woven into modern life. Have students find or write other poems that describe the beauty and interconnectedness of life.

Illustration ©1993 by Frank Howell from Spirit Walker *by Nancy Wood. Illustrations by Frank Howell. Used by permission of Bantam Doubleday Dell Books for Young Readers.*

Take a Look: An Introduction to the Experience of Art

Rosemary Davidson. Illustrated with photographs. Viking. ISBN 0-670-84478-0. TC '95.

Why do we see what we see when we look at a work of art? Davidson does a thorough and fascinating exploration of the concept that art is an expression of personal choice and experiences, and that viewing art is influenced by our own histories and personalities. Aesthetic and practical in its approach, this book prompts thought-provoking questions about the role of art in our life. It inspires curiosity about the entire selection process that leads to a work of art and about the person who creates it. This book is for all ages.

🐛 *Take a Look* should not be confined to an art history class. It could be helpful in social studies, to examine the ways that art reflects the history of a period or a people; in science, where students could explore why certain materials are chosen to create art; or in any class when a teacher is helping students appreciate themselves as individuals. The book can be used to discuss and learn about the ways the eye and the imagination interact to see the world around them. Teachers can use this book to inspire more careful observations of art and of everyday events. Children will begin to use a variety of media with greater understanding and appreciation as they produce their own artwork.

Tell Them We Remember: The Story of the Holocaust

Susan D. Bachrach. Illustrated with photographs from the United States Holocaust Memorial Museum. Little, Brown. ISBN 0-316-69264-6. TC '95.

> This is a complete explanation of the Holocaust with heart-rending photographs. It describes how the Holocaust affected the daily lives of innocent people throughout Europe. It also includes a good introduction to the U.S. Holocaust Memorial Museum.
>
> ❦ This is a useful resource for the study of World War II and the impact of genocide, along with Maxine B. Rosenberg's *Hiding to Survive* (Teachers' Choice 1995) and related titles. By learning about the Holocaust, we will be able to tell the victims we remember.

A Time of Angels

Karen Hesse. Hyperion. ISBN 0-7868-0087-9. TC '96.

> Fourteen-year-old Hannah's Jewish family is torn apart during World War I. The struggle to survive an influenza epidemic and other adversities make this a story of warm friendship and compassion.
>
> ❦ This book is a useful supplement to the study of World War I. Students might research other deadly disease epidemics or interview elderly citizens who lived through this period.

The Underground Railroad

Raymond Bial. Illustrated with photographs. Houghton Mifflin. ISBN 0-395-69937-1. TC '96.

> Photographs in this work show actual places and artifacts that were a part of the slaves' secret escape route. The narrative recounts interesting facts about the Underground Railroad.
>
> ❦ During a study of slavery and the U.S. Civil War, students might keep an illustrated diary or journal as though they were a part of the Underground Railroad.

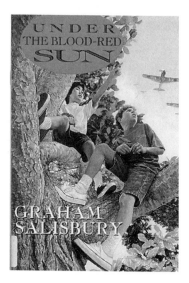

From Under the Blood-Red
Sun *by Graham Salisbury.*
©1994 by Graham Salisbury.
*Used by permission of
Delacorte Press, a division of
Bantam Doubleday Dell
Publishing Group, Inc.*

Under the Blood-Red Sun

Graham Salisbury. Delacorte. ISBN 0-385-32099-X. TC '95.

> Baseball, ocean fishing, and Hawaiian sunshine—sounds
> peaceful. But this is Honolulu in September 1941, and the
> mortal storm of war, seen through the amazed eyes of eighth
> grader Tomi Nakaji, is about to disrupt Oahu and the world.
> Both funny and heart-rending, this historical fiction is by an
> assured new writer.
>
> ✿ Read the book aloud, interspersing with Readers Theatre,
> to give a humanistic perspective on the political events of
> World War II. Have students compare the headings to maps
> of the island and surrounding ocean to introduce attributes of
> historical fiction.

Wilma Mankiller

Caroline Lazo. Illustrated with photographs. Dillon.
ISBN 0-87518-635-1. TC '95.

> Intermediate readers may have some understanding of the
> ravages history has taken on the Native American nations,
> but little has been written about efforts to reclaim lost rights
> and restore cultural pride. Lazo portrays Wilma Mankiller as
> the Dr. Martin Luther King, Jr., of her people; her story
> deserves a place in any classroom library. The book is an

excellent reinforcement of both American Indian history and present-day culture.

🎭 Wilma Mankiller presents a positive role model for young people, particularly minorities, who are interested in politics. Use the book to study the intricacies of U.S. politics, the lives of famous women leaders, and multicultural appreciation. Encourage students to seek out similar biographies. Have students keep written journals, complete with news clippings, on prominent political figures they admire.

With Every Drop of Blood
James Lincoln Collier and Christopher Collier. Delacorte. ISBN 0-385-32028-0. TC '95.

A broken promise leads a young white boy into a world where roles are reversed and extreme changes are being forced on the population of the U.S. South at the end of the Civil War. Slaves are free and free men are prisoners. Cooperation and education are the only avenues to rebuilding shattered lives, families, and the nation.

🎭 Students could transform the map at the front of the book into a large "pictomap" showing major incidents from the book and from the rest of the war. The concluding section of the book—"How Much of This Book Is True?"— could be applied to other historical fiction.

From With Every Drop of Blood by James Lincoln Collier and Christopher Collier ©1994. Used by permission of Bantam Doubleday Dell Books for Young Readers.

Author and Illustrator Index

58

Title Index

The International Reading Association attempts, through its publications, to provide a forum for a wide spectrum of opinions on reading. This policy permits divergent viewpoints without implying the endorsement of the Association.

Director of Publications   Joan M. Irwin
Assistant Director of Publications   Wendy Lapham Russ
Managing Editor, Books and Electronic Publications   Christian A. Kempers
Associate Editor   Matthew W. Baker
Assistant Editor   Janet S. Parrack
Editorial Coordinator   Cynthia C. Sawaya
Association Editor   David K. Roberts
Production Department Manager   Iona Sauscermen
Graphic Design Coordinator   Boni Nash
Electronic Publishing Supervisor   Wendy A. Mazur
Electronic Publishing Specialist   Anette Schütz-Ruff
Electronic Publishing Specialist   Cheryl J. Strum
Electronic Publishing Assistant   Peggy Mason

Photo Credits   Cover Photo: Lloyd Wolf
                   Cover Design: Larry Husfelt

SUPPLEMENT:
TEACHERS' CHOICES
in the
Classroom

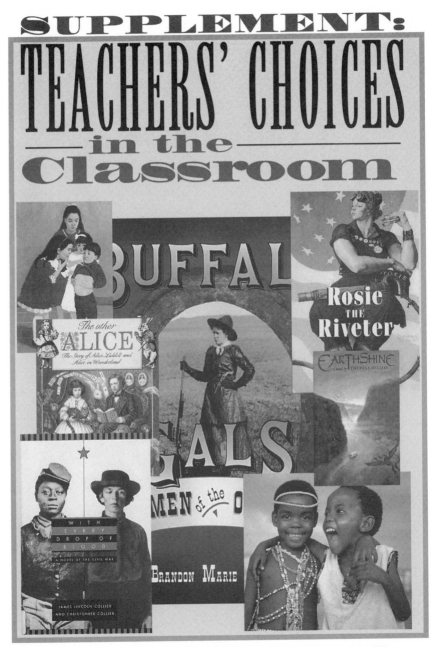

Illustrations from (from top left): *Too Many Tamales; Buffalo Gals: Women of the Old West; Rosie the Riveter: Women Working on the Home Front in World War II; Earthshine; My Painted House, My Friendly Chicken, and Me; With Every Drop of Blood;* and *The Other Alice: The Story of Alice Liddell and Alice in Wonderland.*

Contents

Introduction: The Power of Books—The Power of Teachers

Carole S. Rhodes

The author is an associate professor of education at Pace University in Pleasantville, New York, USA.

When I was first asked to write this piece, I thought I would call it "The Power of Books," but the Teachers' Choices project involves more than just books. A key element in this project is the teachers. This project acknowledges teachers as vital in fostering students' transactions with literature. It recognizes the importance of students, of high-quality literature, and of curricular connections. My involvement with the International Reading Association Teachers' Choices project has spanned almost a decade, beginning with an application to be a regional coordinator and culminating with a three-year stint as chair of the project and editor of this special insert. These have been extraordinary professional experiences.

The IRA Teachers' Choices project recognizes the importance of classroom teachers in the book selection process. It acknowledges books of high literary quality that relate to students and the curriculum. The compilation presented in this book represents the work of hundreds of classroom teachers from across the country who read and reviewed thousands of titles. This special insert, written by teachers who have served as coordinators, team leaders, or readers, evolved from a Preconvention institute, which was presented at the 1997 IRA 42nd Annual Convention in Atlanta, Georgia. Gail Waxman Karpf, Ginnie Schroder, and I were among the speakers who, we are told, captivated participants as we and others discussed how we used Teachers' Choices books in our classrooms. We discussed the books and our students as we showed samples of students' responses and the multiple curricular connections that were fostered after they read the books.

The annotations in this volume are provided as a brief overview for teachers who are seeking good books for their students. This is just the beginning. Successfully introducing books, connecting books to the students and the curriculum, and encouraging students' responses are the essence of this special insert. It begins with a section on the multiple factors to consider in selecting and evaluating books. Gail Waxman Karpf then shares her experiences as part of a middle school team that incorporates literature across the curriculum. Ginnie Schroder concludes with a piece that discusses poetry and its impression on youngsters.

For the past ten years, the IRA Teachers' Choices project has been instrumental in "getting books into the hands of those who use them"— specifically teachers and students. A special note of appreciation is due Bernice Cullinan, who provided the impetus for the project and who still is an integral part of it. The Teachers' Choices project values teachers as readers and as decision makers. It recognizes the strong influence of teachers and of books. My hands-on involvement with this project is ending. The impact of the project, what it has afforded me and thousands of others, will, like a "good read," stay with us forever.

Evaluating and Selecting Quality Children's Books

Carole S. Rhodes

The Teachers' Choices project recognizes the importance of educators in the book selection process. Knowledgeable teachers can introduce books to their students and foster in them the sense of wonder, enchantment, and knowledge that books provide. Through exposure to material high in literary and aesthetic quality, readers become more discerning and develop a strong appreciation for well-written stories (Glazer, 1997). These experiences are key to the development of lifelong readers who love reading and recognize good literature. Inherent in the teacher's role is a recognition of the value of literature-based instruction and a dedication to facilitating its use in classrooms.

Children often do not discover great books on their own. Neither do most adults. Administrators, parents, teachers, and library media specialists all can help students discover books. There are many resources available for adults as they pursue their quest to find quality books for children. The selection of books is, to a large measure, contingent upon an awareness of books available. Lists, reviews, and annotations are very helpful, but they are just starting points. These resources should serve as

Adapted by permission of the publisher from Wepner, S.B., Feeley, J.T., & Strickland, D.S. (Eds.), *The administration and supervision of reading programs* (2nd ed., pp. 111–129). New York: Teachers College Press, ©1995 by Teachers College, Columbia University. All rights reserved.

guides, not mandates (Feeley & Rhodes, 1995). Those who are instrumental in recommending or selecting books for youngsters must read them first. To select books for their students, teachers should consider three major elements: the readers, the books, and the curriculum. The following sections provide an in-depth look at some criteria to consider when selecting books for children and young adults.

The selection of books must begin with an awareness of the reader. Knowledge of the prior life and literary experiences of the reader are crucial as we try to foster and facilitate a child's transactions with text. In her seminal work, Rosenblatt (1938/1976) describes the literary experience as one in which a "live circuit" is activated as a reader's mind intersects with a text. This live circuit is further developed when readers encounter books that relate to their lives or their experiences. For example, an African American adolescent from an inner city found close connections to his life in Eve Bunting's *The Blue and the Gray*, although the book takes place during the Civil War, as shown in his response:

> It was like where I live, neighbor to neighbor, we can be friends or we can destroy each other. This is way cool. I can really get into this stuff, it's real, it's mine.

Jane Yolen's *Grandad Bill's Song* resonated for one young woman, as can be seen in the following excerpt from her response journal:

> When my uncle died, I was afraid to talk about him. Everyone was so upset, and I didn't want to upset them even more. But this boy was able to talk to everyone about his dead grandfather and that made me wish that I could "hear my uncle's song."

To promote a "good match" between a reader and a text, it is important to be aware of the various stages of development within and among readers. To facilitate this match best, a teacher must have a keen sense of both the reader and the text. Many professional books and journal articles contain interest inventories that teachers can use to discover information about their students' interests and preferences. Teachers can develop their own resources that help them know their students better. Informal discussions and observations often provide insight into students' favorite hobbies, aspirations, talents, and interests. A thoughtful adult can discern that which the youngsters can handle emotionally. All this information will be invaluable in promoting students' active engagement with literature. The figure on the next page includes questions

Who are the readers?
> What are their interests
> Do they have hobbies?
> Do they have any special talents?
> Do they enjoy sports, fantasy, or history?
> What are their favorite movies or television shows?
> What type of video games do they favor?

What reading background do they bring?
> Are they readers who willingly read?
> Do they see reading as a pleasurable activity?
> What genres have intriguied them?

What books do they like?
> Do they favor realism, fantasy, or adventure?
> Do they read series books?

What books do they dislike?
> Do they shun books with sad endings?
> Do they shy away from books dealing with social issues?

What can they read independently?
What can they handle emotionally?

about readers that teachers may want to consider as they begin to select books for their students.

Through books, readers enter secondary, often new worlds. These worlds provide opportunities for readers to ponder issues, examine different roles and identities, and gain information. A book that has high literary quality will actively engage students and foster aesthetic and efferent reading. Criteria for high-quality literature mandates that books have well-developed plots, themes, characterizations, and settings, and that the author uses language that is rich and is consistent with the content of the book. We need to look for books that youngsters can read and enjoy. The figure on the next page provides an overview of some questions to consider that focus on the books.

Thousands of books are published yearly, and there are many resources to help in an initial exploration. Many awards for exemplary books are given annually. The Newbery Award, given to an author based on literary quality of a text, and the Caldecott Award, given to the illus-

Guidelines for Selecting Trade Books: Focus on the Books

Do the books represent high literary quality?
   Evaluate the author's use of plot structure, characterization, setting, theme, style, and language.
   Is the story engaging?
What books are within students' reading ability?
What books relate to students' experiential background?
What books are currently being read?
   Do they read only certain types of books? Do they read only series books or comic books?
What authors have they enjoyed?
What books connect with their lives?
What authors' works are worth pursuing?
   Are books readily available?
   Can we gain information about the authors?
Would the books engage the reader?
Are stereotypes and generalizations avoided?

trator of the most distinguished picture book, are administered by the American Library Association. The American Library Association also selects honor books each year. The Hans Christian Andersen Awards, given biannually to both an author and illustrator for significant contributions to children's literature, are presented by the International Board on Books for Young People. In addition, organizations such as the International Reading Association and the National Council of Teachers of English give awards to exemplary books.

Conversations with colleagues, attendance at conferences, and special newspaper supplements all provide opportunities to learn about newly published books. Book reviews are published in journals such as *The Journal of Children's Literature; The School Library Journal, The Reading Teacher*, and *The Journal of Adolescent & Adult Literacy*. These peer-reviewed journals give educators a wealth of information about new books as well as earlier books still in print. Many articles in these journals explore ways to integrate literature and expand its use within and across the curriculum.

The incorporation of trade books in the curriculum involves more than just finding books that detail or provide specific curricular-relevant information. Trade books should be an integral part of the curriculum and should be used to enhance curricular studies. The impact of literature-based instruction is evident in the words of Greg, a fifth-grade student whose class was studying the U.S. Revolutionary War. Greg read James L. Collier and Christopher Collier's *My Brother Sam in Dead*, a story set in revolutionary times that deals with a family as it struggles with conflicting loyalties. Initially, only two youngsters opted to read the book. Greg read the book in two days, and when he came into school, he was excited. He proclaimed to all who would listen, "I was there, I was in the war." He eagerly detailed *his* experiences in the war. His enthusiasm was infectious; others opted to read the book and their reactions were similar. Their knowledge of the Revolutionary War increased as did their interest in historical fiction (Feeley & Rhodes, 1995). A few years later while studying the Holocaust, Greg sought out books such as *Star of Fear, Star of Hope*; *Hiding to Survive: Stories of Jewish Children Rescued from the Holocaust*; and *Tell Them We Remember: The Story of the Holocaust*. Greg, now a 17-year-old, still relates to these earlier literary experiences as he studies.

Well-selected trade books can be a valuable resource for all content-area teachers. When contemplating the integration and incorporation of trade books across the curriculum, key curricular and literary issues must be explored, which are highlighted in the figure on the following page. An integrated thematic approach is greatly enhanced by giving students opportunities to read books that provide multiple perspectives, varied viewpoints, and a wide body of knowledge. Fiction and nonfiction can supplement and stimulate students' interest and knowledge. The prime responsibility for evaluating the veracity of the trade books lies with the adults with whom the student interacts. Books that contain authentic, accurate, honest, and culturally sensitive portrayals and information can stimulate minds as they provide direct experiences within a contextual base.

Louise Rosenblatt described the powerful transaction that forms the basis of reading. Through books, readers explore new worlds, ponder issues, learn information, consider multiple perspectives, and continually expand and modify their horizons. It is necessary for educators to provide opportunities for students to experience life through high-quality literature. Classrooms should be safe harbors that cultivate divergent responses, encourage reflection, and foster the love of literature. I hope

Do the books present multiple perspectives?
Do the books stimulate divergent responses?
Do the illustrations and text accurately portray the topic?
Is the content of the books accurate?
Will the books capture students' interest?
Will the books foster sharing of ideas, experiences, and thoughts?
How can books be incorporated into the curriculum?
How might the books expand the curriculum?
What aspects of the curriculum will be enhanced through the use of trade books?
What can readers learn through reading the book?
   Is there specific subject matter information?
   Can the reader learn more about the world through the reading?
Are the books accessible?

---

that the suggestions offered here will help educators plan positive literary and learning experiences for the children and young adults with whom they work.

References

Feeley, J.T., & Rhodes, C.S. (1995). A new look at the materials selection process. In S.B. Wepner, J.T. Feeley, & D.S. Strickland (Eds.), *The administration and supervision of reading* (2nd ed., pp. 111–129). New York: Teachers College Press; Newark, DE: International Reading Association.

Glazer, J. (1997). *Introduction to children's literature.* New York: Merrill.

Rosenblatt, L. (1976). *Literature as exploration.* (3rd ed.). New York: Modern Language Association. (Original work published 1938)

Children's Literature Cited

Bachrach, S. (1995). *Tell them we remember: The story of the Holocaust.* New York: Little, Brown.

Bunting, E. (1996). *The Blue and the gray* (N. Bittinger, Ill.). New York: Scholastic.

Collier, J.L., & Collier, C. (1974). *My brother Sam is dead.* New York: Macmillan.

Hoestlandt, J. (1996). *Star of fear, star of hope* (J. Kand, Ill.). New York: Walker.

Rosenberg, M. (1995). *Hiding to survive: Stories of Jewish children rescued from the Holocaust.* New York: Clarion.

Yolen, J. (1995). *Grandad Bill's song* (M. Mathis, Ill.). New York: Philomel.

Team Teaching Using Teachers' Choices Books

Gail Waxman Karpf

The author teaches fifth and sixth grade at Poly Prep Country Day School in Brooklyn, New York, USA.

Being part of a core group of teachers is akin to being part of a highly complex piece of machinery. Each person on the team has a clearly defined role in the larger picture, one that does not need to be written, one that has evolved over numerous hours of planning over the past seven years. Our language has become an unspoken one; a certain glance or a particular movement can read volumes. We truly have become a well-oiled machine. And whether we are sharing lunches, a slice of birthday cake, a walk around our school's track, or a well-deserved dinner out, we ultimately speak about our shared family, the fifth and sixth graders we all teach—the fuel that keeps us running.

I serve as the reading teacher for the fifth grade, focusing on literature and all its wonders. To sixth graders, I am their English teacher, the one who introduces them to the writing process, grammar, vocabulary, public speaking, and poetry. Anastasia (Annie) Nakos is the English teacher for the fifth graders and the reading teacher for sixth graders. In this way, the middle school students in our school get nine periods of language arts weekly, something we consider to be a great advantage. Liane Dougherty is our social studies specialist. Marie Corkhill is our

S11

science scholar, and Kathleen (Kate) Flahive, our math wizard. Careful construction of schedules has afforded us the opportunity to have at least two periods each day when we are all free—free to meet and discuss students, upcoming events, the trials and tribulations of daily middle school life—but most important, it gives us the opportunity to create curriculum.

Ideas for the curriculum come to us from many places (workshops, conferences, and education journals), but our latest course of study came to us via Kate Flahive's recent summer vacation in Oregon. While at the Sun River resort, she and her family met Jerry Sodoris, who, along with his sled dogs, entertained the guests at the resort. After meeting Mr. Sodoris, the Flahive family visited his training ground, one that is used by mushers to train their teams for the Alaskan Iditarod. It was this experience that prompted Kate to bring a bit of the Iditarod to our first planning meeting in September. It didn't take much to convince us that using this annual race as a unit topic would be fun for all.

The webbing process had begun. We had decided that our study would coincide with the actual Iditarod race in March. We made an effort to include activities that involved more than one teacher—this truly would be an interdisciplinary unit. The Internet proved to be a great help, as we were able to download the information we needed such as the names of the mushers, the rules of the race, and weather reports. Musher terminology became part of our everyday vocabulary. Students drew lots out of a boot (the way real mushers determine their position in the Iditarod) and picked a musher, one they would follow throughout the duration of the actual race. We were on our way!

The hallway bulletin boards were inundated with the coming of the Iditarod to our school, rules of the race, photos of the mushers, and a map of the trail. Students were hooked. Off they went to the technology center and the library to gather any information that they could to learn more about Alaska. From the state flag to the state tree, from the names of daily newspapers to photos of native animals, fifth graders had what we referred to as "Iditarod fever."

Students wanted to read, read, read, and that is when the best part of my job began. When Carole Rhodes was regional coordinator of the Teachers' Choices project in our school's area, I had access to a wealth of fine children's literature. Two of these books became a focal point in the Iditarod study: *Woodsong* by Gary Paulsen and *Iditarod Dream: Dusty and His Sled Dogs Compete in Alaska's Junior Iditarod* by Ted Wood.

Woodsong, a true account of Paulsen's relationship with animals and nature, particularly husky dogs, ends with his personal reflections of his Iditarod experience. Students became enthralled, and Paulsen and his dogs became our friends. After completing this book, students expressed great interest in how they could become mushers when they got older. They then read *Iditarod Dream*, a colorfully illustrated book, which tells the true story of a junior musher-in-training, Dusty, who is preparing to run in the Junior Iditarod, a race for 17- and 18-year-olds. Reading this book led to many creative activities. Students kept Musher's journals containing activities to stretch their imaginations. They collected trading cards, wrote diary entries in the voices of mushers and dogs and letters to Gary Paulsen, and engaged in the following activities:

1. Create a catalog of items that would be needed for the Iditarod. Be sure to include the appropriate food, clothing, and supplies. Sketch each of the necessary items and write a few sentences to describe each item below the sketch. Here is an example from Alicia's catalog:

> Buy this new and incredible sleeping bag. It is so warm that when it is 40 degrees below zero, you will be sweating in it. This sleeping bag comes in blue, green, and red. It also comes with a pillow, just in case the ground is hard. The pillow only comes in a medium size. The price for both of these items is only $89.95. Call today, as supplies are limited.

2. Dusty lived his Iditarod dream. Write your own Iditarod dream poem.

Scenes from the two books often were dramatized and analyzed, leading sometimes to moral questions: Are dogs treated fairly in the Iditarod? When is it time to quit? How difficult is it to train a team of dogs? Questions like these could be heard in many of the fifth-grade classrooms. In social studies class, Liane Dougherty spoke about the history of the race: "Did you know that the trail was used in the days of the Gold Rush? Did you know that the Iditarod we know today, actually was created by Dorothy Page and Joe Reddington? Mr. Reddington, 80-years-young, competed in the race this year, as did his son, Joe Reddington, Jr." These facts were shared as students worked busily on maps of Alaska, highlighting the land areas as well as important cities and industries.

In Annie Nakos's English class, Inuit myths or folk tales were being told or dramatized. Her students wrote letters to a class of fifth graders in Shaktoolik, a small community on Norton Sound. Approximately 200 people live in this area, where most of them make their living by fishing.

Their school is located close to one of the Iditarod checkpoints. There were so many questions to ask the Alaskan fifth graders: How do you celebrate the arrival of the mushers? Can you actually speak to the mushers? Are you allowed to pet any of the dogs? The list went on and on. All questions were answered in May, when letters arrived from Alaska. We learned that the Iditarod is a very exciting time for the children of Shaktoolik. Mushers check in at the local armory and care for their own dogs. Years ago villagers were allowed to help, but this is no longer so. Students, however, spend time talking to mushers and petting their dogs. Some mushers give candy to the children. Booties (foot protection for the sled dogs) are collected by the students after the race and later used in activities such as math games.

Meanwhile, back in our school, the math room became the headquarters for learning the mapping skills necessary to compete in this special event. Studies about latitude, longitude, and the proper use of a compass were carefully coordinated by Kate Flahive. Students would move around the room following the directions given, traveling through trails as if they were actual mushers. Word problems focused on statistics, such as the population of Alaska compared with other states. Excitement was everywhere as students created math board games that highlighted the actual trail from Anchorage to Nome. Game pieces were created using various materials from clay and cardboard to wood and plastic. Boards clearly illustrated the checkpoints that would serve as rest stops along the way. Cards with messages such as "one dog lost a bootie, lose a turn" were included. After playing these games in class, they became a favorite activity during free times.

Marie Corkhill's science room, however, was where the "Ikidarod" was born. After explaining the rules of the actual Iditarod to students, material was downloaded from the Internet that contained information about Iditarod simulations done in schools around the country. This inspired Marie to design a trail over the land surrounding our school. After teaching students about cold-weather survival, students were able to answer questions such as, "Why is layered clothing the best to wear?" or "What materials will keep mushers warmest?" A study of cold-weather nutrition led to queries such as, "What are the best foods to eat on such a strenuous journey?" "Why is gorp (trail mix) a good food to carry with you?" Adaptations of Northern breeds of dogs (Malamutes, Samoyeds, and Huskies) were studied as well, leading to a study of the design and contents of sleds. Speculation as to the contents carried on mushers' sleds and the designs of the sleds used in the actual race was a perfect introduction to the first annual Ikidarod at our school.

Once again, a boot was used to draw sticks in order to create teams of seven or eight people, with one person serving as a musher and the others as sled dogs. Teams then chose names: Ice Pirates, Icebreakers, Moon Wolves, Alaskids, and Sliders. Mushers were picked by voting within the individual teams. The following tasks had to be done by each team: bibs needed to be made for each musher and dog, booties needed to be made for each dog, and a sled had to be created—one that could be dragged by the team or carried by a dog or musher. Each sled had to be able to hold booties, water bottles for each dog as well as one for the musher, a bag of food containing enough to feed both the dogs and the musher at specific checkpoints, a harness (rope), and a repair kit for the sled and the harness (tape and scissors).

The trail map of our school was distributed to mushers, and check-point areas were carefully labeled Rocky Road, Maple Hill, Apple Grove, and North and South Glaciers. The day before the race, all fifth-grade students and teachers walked around the trail to become familiar with the terrain. Sixth-grade students were assigned positions at checkpoints: the places where all teams were required to sign in, feed their dogs, check the condition of booties, and rest.

The day of the race was cold and windy, as dogs and mushers bundled up for the big event. Cooperation and teamwork abounded. One team's sled, a cardboard box, fell apart and the team had to forfeit. Others trudged along as booties fell off and had to be reapplied (plastic bags seemed to work best). Adults ensured that mandatory rests were made. Teachers, dressed as moose, wolves, and bears, carried water guns, which were used as obstacles. They were, however, subject to bribes with snacks such as trail mix and corn chips. At the conclusion, our weary, yet exhilarated travelers returned to the starting point to celebrate their success. We all gathered to share our experiences and feelings about the events of the past three weeks. When students were asked what they would like to do as a follow-up activity, all agreed on two tasks: (1) to write letters to Gary Paulsen telling him about their study, and (2) to write thank you notes to their musher or dogs. Douglas, one of the mushers, wrote the following letter to Gary Paulsen on the next page.

Dear Mr. Paulsen,

My name is Douglas and I go to school in New York City. I just read your book *Woodsong* for a unit on the Iditarod. I represent the race we have run an "Ikidarod." In this race, the fifth grade brought in supplies (a bib to tell which group we were in, booties, and a sled). These items could have been made from many different materials.

Woodsong is the best book I have ever read. My favorite part was when Columbia pushed the bone just out of the reach of Olaf. I just couldn't put this book down. I read it whenever I had the chance. Thanks so much for writing it.

Sincerely,

Douglas

When students were asked if they would do anything differently the next time, they unanimously agreed that the study should be longer, a few months perhaps. We are considering that for next year. All the children look forward to working at checkpoints and aiding the incoming fifth graders. As for the teachers involved, we already are preparing for next year's study.

Children's Literature Cited

Paulsen, G. (1990). *Woodsong*. New York: Bradbury Press/Macmillan.
Wood, T. (1996). *Iditarod dream: Dusty and his sled dogs compete in Alaska's Junior Iditarod*. New York: Walker.

Poetry: The Teachers' Choice

Ginnie Schroder

The author teaches third grade in the Manhasset Public Schools, Manhasset, New York, USA. She served as the Northeast Teachers' Choices Regional Coordinator from 1993 to 1995.

In every year of the International Reading Association Teachers' Choices project, since its inception in 1989, there have been books of poetry among the 30 books selected annually by teachers across the country. I think that this trend is due to teachers' recognition and appreciation of the poet's craft, that miraculous ability to sculpt language to reveal the essence of a memory, an idea, or an emotion. Teachers also acknowledge the need children have for poetry in their lives—a need that is never outgrown. Indeed, children are poets first. They play with language as they learn it, repeating words, inventing words to make rhymes when they can't think of another way, turning their phrases into songs that they hum to themselves, and using words they don't understand just because they like the way they fall off the tongue or roll around in the mouth. Children are image makers, too. They invent invisible words, impossible situations, and imaginary people, so they are bound to love the imagination and creativity that is embedded in poetry.

Poetry appeals to children when it's introduced to them naturally and with enjoyment. Its rhythm can be a heady pace—a gallop from word to word, or heart-paced and steady, or lyrical and waltz-like. *Paul Revere's Ride* by Longfellow moves with the sound of hoof beats; "Song of the Builders," from *Celebrate America in Poetry and Art* edited by Panzer, echoes with the staccato of a jack hammer; and "Poems," from

Inner Chimes: Poems on Poetry by Goldstein, rocks with the gentle rhythm of a boat on the water.

The rhyme of a poem can be a surprise or it can be predictable and expected. The predictability allows young readers to fill in the blank at the end of a rhyming line and feel successful when we share poems with them—such as the nursery rhyme "High Diddle, Diddle, the Cat and the Fiddle..." from *If There Were Dreams to Sell* by Lalicki.

Poetry's repetition is something to hold on to and remember. It draws in the listener and the reader, almost making them a part of the poem. "The Little Turtle," by Lindsey in *Sing a Song of Popcorn: Every Child's Book of Poems* is an easy first poem because of its anticipated repetition as it tells a story. This is a wonderful poem for early primary children because they can say it by heart after hearing it read just a few times.

Beginning readers thrive on poetry. As they listen and learn to join in the reading of poems, they are developing phonemic awareness and good listening skills. They are learning to make predictions about what comes next—a strategy all good readers use—and they are learning the power and music of words. Poetry can introduce new words and new worlds and help children see the commonplace in different ways—as in the poem "Seahorse," from *Words with Wrinkled Knees"* edited by Esbensen.

Poetry also makes us aware of beautiful prose. It teaches ears to listen, eyes to see, and voices to sing. In poetry there is laughter and tears, wild adventure, and cozy calm.

There is an abundance of fine poetry for children available today, making it easy to gather poems tailored for the special needs and individual interests of children. You can find a poem about almost any subject—especially in a collection of Teachers' Choices poetry books.

Poetry should be shared first for the pleasure it brings—its rhythm, its visual imagery, and the emotional response it evokes. Its use in the classroom should be natural: a part of everything else that is occurring, rather than a separate unit of study in which it is dissected for meaning, memorized, or used as a writing exercise. Poems used through the grades should include free verse and rhymed verse, ballads, Haiku, concrete poems, limericks, and what Kennedy calls "word music" in *Knock at a Star: A Child's Introduction to Poetry*. Most of all, poetry is meant to be heard!

In a first-grade classroom I visited, the students were working on the drafts of their last books for the school year. They selected topics to write about from favorite school memories or from happenings outside of school. One youngster was writing about the birth of his baby sister.

Another was retelling all the current events the class has discussed. Still another was writing about living in London for two years.

The teacher noticed that several of the students had created a pattern for their writing. For example, Kathy used an "I can be" structure in her writing: "I can be anything when I grow up. I can be a doctor and take care of people. I can be a dentist and take care of people's teeth. I can be an astronaut and fly to the moon and Mars." Kyle began an "I Spy" book, with objects hidden in his illustrations. Some of his pages rhymed, and he liked the way that sounded. Drew was writing "My Backyard Poetry Book." Each page told something that was happening in either unrhymed or rhyming verse.

These children know poetry. They have read it and heard it read since kindergarten. They have favorite poems and poets. They can identify the rhymes and poetic styles they have used in their writing. Their writing demonstrates a sense of rhythm and language use that they have borrowed from many sources of poetry.

When I visited this classroom to work with a group of children who wanted their writing pieces to look like poetry, I brought with me David McCord's *All Small* and Eric Carle's *Animals, Animals*. We looked at line breaks and white spaces and talked about what effect they have on a reader and the shape of the poem. We talked about the surprise a poet can elicit just by putting a word by itself on a line, by capitalizing every letter in a word, or by snaking a word down a page. We read several poems aloud to confirm our observations. Then we returned to the story drafts they brought with them.

Kathy believed that her "I can be" statements would look more like poetry if she created line breaks at the end of certain repeated phrases. She drew slashes between words in her draft and began a new draft to see how her line breaks would look on paper. Next, she copied the shape of a poem from one of the books we shared, indenting as she wrote— each line just a bit more than the one above it. Kathy decided that she liked this effect and continued it as she wrote her new draft.

Drew's decisions about his poem were quite different. He listened carefully as we took turns reading his piece aloud. Whenever he heard a natural break in the text, he drew a slash to indicate the start of a new line. Drew noticed that poets can do unusual things to make their poems interesting and to capture the reader's eye. Poets can ignore conventional rules of writing, so Drew decided to put a single word on a line in several places and to write the word in capital letters to show its importance in the poem.

Kyle started his "I Spy" piece as prose but switched to rhyming couplets after several pages. He decided to make every page rhyme and went back to the beginning of his draft to rewrite each nonrhyming page. He realized that he also had to change the illustrations to match his new copy. "I spy a red boat, a yellow hat, a pair of dice, and a black bat."

The ease with which the first graders I worked with revised their written work and turned them into wonderful books with rhymes, repetition, and shapes on a page could only have been achieved after they had been immersed in poetry. Their astonishing dedication to their work showed in the number of drafts they were willing to write—three or four drafts of a 16-page book was not unusual. In fact, it was difficult to persuade some of the children to stop for snack time when they were writing! Several days later, once they had their poems just as they wanted them to be, they copied them into hardcover blank books and carefully illustrated them. The books were completed with a dedication page and a page about the author. Finally, they invited their parents for a special Author's Day celebration.

Teachers' Choices poetry books helped shape writers' workshop for these students even before they began to write words and sentences. Poetry gave them the language tools they needed to become authors with a strong sense of voice and an intense devotion to the power of words on a page. Share the gift of poetry. Make it a goal that every child in your classroom knows its wide range of topics and many styles and shapes. Let each child hear and read enough poetry to be able to identify at least one favorite poem or poet, and provide your students with enough writing time so that they have plenty of opportunities to write using a poet's voice.

Children's Literature Cited

Carle, E. (1989). *Animals, animals.* New York: Philomel.

High Diddle, Diddle. (1985). In B. Lalicki (Ed.), *If there were dreams to sell.* New York: Lothrop, Lee, & Shepard.

Kennedy, X.J., & Kennedy, D.M. (Eds.). (1982). *Knock at a star: A child's introduction to poetry.* New York: Little, Brown.

Lindsey, V. (1988). The little turtle. In E. Moore, *Sing a song of popcorn: Every child's book of poems.* New York: Scholastic.

Longfellow, H.W. (1990). *Paul Revere's ride.* New York: Dutton.

McCord, D. (1986). *All small.* New York: Little, Brown.

Poems. (1992). In B.S. Goldstein (Ed.), *Inner chimes: Poems on poetry.* Honesdale, PA: Wordsong/Boyds Mill Press.

Seahorse. (1987). In B.J. Esbensen (Ed.), *Words with wrinkled knees.* New York: Crowell Jr. Books/HarperCollins.

Song of the builders. (1995). In N. Panzer (Ed.), *Celebrate America in poetry and art.* New York: Hyperion.